Carlo Cestra

Schnellboot Type S-38 and S-100

KAGERO

Schnellboot S38B, 1942.
Starboard side.

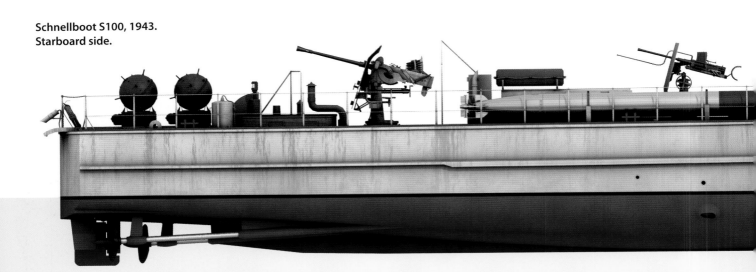

Schnellboot S100, 1943.
Starboard side.

Overview

S38b and S100 E-boats class were german fast attack craft (Schnellboot in german) built for the Kriegsmarine during World War Two.

The E-boats (a British designation using the letter E for Enemy) were defined by many naval experts as the best carrying out of their category. Initially these units were called Unterseebot Zerstörer (Hunting Submarine) and Anti-Submmarine Motorboats or Armored Motorboats, as they had an important anti-submarine mission. Later the Kaiserliche Marine (imperial german navy) adopted the designation of Luftschiffmotorenboot (boat with an airship engine) or L-Boote and, therefore, from November 1917, the units became LM-Boote, with the same meaning, but their use, especially in the Baltic Sea and the North Sea, was not particularly successful.

After the defeat in the First World War, Germany was subject to heavy military restrictions, sanctioned by the Treaty of Versailles, but the Winning Powers did not consider to put particular attention to the torpedo boats, leaving the Reichsmarine free hand.

In 1923 the Reichsmarine entrusted the Captain of vessel Walter Lohmann and the Lieutenant of vessel Friedrich Ruge to start a program of development of fast coastal units, hiding the projects under cover codes and applying to private technical offices. Their activity went unnoticed by the Allied Armistice Control Commission, but not by the parliamentary opposition, which opposed the rearmament of

Germany, and in 1928 Lohmann was forced to resign. New officers and new dummy corporations were quietly put in place soon after the Lhoman scandal and the program went ahead anyway. Already in 1926, the Abeking & Rasmussen studio designed the experimental K-Boot, taking its inspiration from the British Thornycroft Coastal Motor Boat. The result was a motorboat of about 18m in length, with two 450hp petrol engines, armed with two rear-facing 457mm torpedo tubes. At the same time, the Lürssen shipyards built a slightly larger torpedo, designated as Lür, a little less than 20m long and driven by three Maybach 450CV engines. Both these units were carefully evaluated, but the attention of the German Admiralty felt on the Oheka II, a 22.50m "motoryacht" with three 550hp Maybach engines, built by Lürssen for banker Otto Herman Kahn. This boat had a light alloy structure covered in wood and offered excellent sea quality. A unit of this type was ordered by the Reichsmarine in November 1929 as UZ(S)16, that is Unterseeboot Zerstörer (Schnell), but in 1932 it became Schnellboot 1, S-boot 1 or S-1.

The S-1 entered service on 7 August 1930 and since then the Kriegsmarine received a great variety of types and classes of torpedo boats. These small units did not have an individual name and were identified by the prefix S and by a number; the acronym of the first unit of each new class was its name.

After the S-1 prototype four S-2s were built, extremely similar to the previous one but slightly larger and with different detail changes.

The development of the E-boats was characterized by continuous growth and, in fact, the S-7s, which entered service between October 1934 and December 1935, were beautiful motorboats with an extended stem of 4.50m and a displacement of 68t. These boats had a traditional line, with a rather vertical stem but they were not fast enough for the Kriegsmarine. The S-14 class of 1936 was even larger and in 1938 the construction of eight S-18s was started. On the basis of the same project, in 1939 and 1940 four S-26s were built, immediately recognizable by a bow castle that hid the two 533mm torpedo tubes, giving the bow of these units a characteristic appearance that will be maintained by all successive classes. While the S-26s were in production, Lürssen developed a new type at the request of China, based on the design of some S-7 class ships. It was the S-30, a slightly smaller boat but the German government blocked the sale and the Kriegsmarine appropriated the first eight units and obtained eight more, all with a modified bow to incorporate the torpedo launchers.

The production of the S-26 taken up in 1939 with a new version, the S-38, with some modifications and variations.

The subclass S-38b, was the result of a mature and highly effective project, with a length of about 35m, a standard displacement of 84t and 104t at full load, and the distinctive armored Kalotte.

With only a few modifications, the S 38 class gave life, in 1943, to the S-100, built in 81 units, some of which had experimental modifications.

With the eight S-151s they returned to much smaller units, that were the Gusto, dutch torpedo boats, produced under English license. These units had been captured incomplete in Netherlands, in May 1940 and were subsequently completed.

Design, propulsion and armor

The E-boats design was chosen because the theatre of operations of such boats was expected to be the North Sea, English Channel and the Western Approaches. The requirement for good performance in rough seas dictated the use of a round-bottomed displacement hull rather than the flat-bottomed planing hull that was more usual for small, high-speed boats.

Construction of the S38b and S100 class hulls started with a keel made from heavy oak bolted together. The hull's longitudinals were made from either Oregon and Scotch pine. Around the engines, pine was replaced by oak. The alluminium alloy frames were spaced at intervals of 575mm (22.6 inch). The pine longitudinals were bolted to the frames, then diagonal stringers were riveted to the frames. Bulkheads were designed to withstand flooding and light splinter damage and they were stiffened with alluminium bracing. Seven bulkheads separated eight waterlight compartments. The engine foundations were made of steel.

**Schnellboot S38B, 1942.
Portside.**

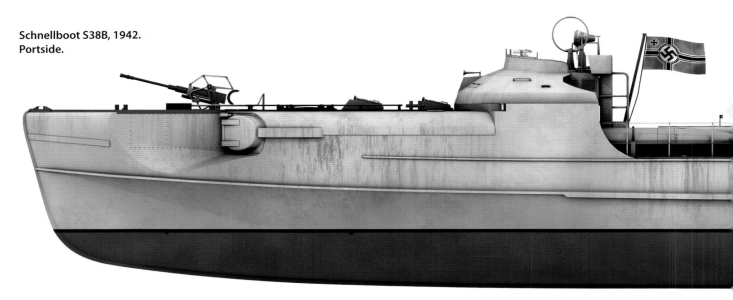

**Schnellboot S100, 1943.
Portside.**

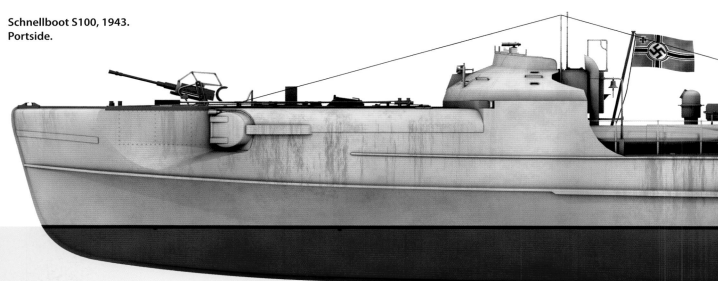

The early S38s were similar to the S26s but they were continuously modified according to experience. They finalized the ventilation arrangement with three large type ventilators over the engines and a significant design change was an increase in firepower to counter steadily increasing enemy MTBs and MGBs opposition. All the modifications were not uniforme and were made according to the needs of the boats' deployment area.

S-38b hulls, built by Vegesack's Lürssen, by the Schlichtling shipyards of Travemünde, by the Taste of Schiedam (in the Netherlands) and by the Danziger Waggonfabrik from Gdansk, were made of oak and pine wood with light aluminum alloy trims, with some steel bulkheads, and steel supports of the engines. The outer part of the hull was in cedar and mahogany wood, while the bridge was in Oregon pine wood covered with painted canvas.

The armored dome, called "Kalotte" (skull cap) was standardized in late 1942 on the S38b, due to increasing casualties among bridge crews and all these E-boats were delidered from the yards with the armored Kalotte fitted in place.

S-38b class was 35 m (114 ft – 10 in) long, with a beam of 5,1 m (16 ft 9 in) and a draught of 1,5 m (5 ft).

S-38b had a propulsion system consisting of three Daimler-Benz MB 511 12-cylinder, liquid cooled, 2200CV that allowed a maximum speed of 39.5 knots. These engines were, in practice, the MB 501 Diesel with 20 V-cylinders equipped with mechanical superchargers that increased its power to 2500CV.

S38b class typically had a crew of up to 30 officers and enlisted men.

Construction of the S38b class continued until july of 1943, when this design was superseded by the S100 Class.

S100s had a new design that began commissioning in mid 1943, similar to the previous S38 class but with a second type of Kalotte (skull cap bridge covering), bow gun tub and additional armor plate provided for the engine superchargers. S100s kept the external dimensions of the S38 class (35 m long, beam of 5,1 m, draught of 1,5 m) and they displaced 100 tons (91 mt) standard and 117 tons (106mt) at full load. The powerplant consisted of three 2500 hp Daimler-Benz MB511 supercharged diesel engines, that enabled the e-boats to reach a maximum speed of 42 knots (48 mph / 78 kmh).

S100 class has an open bridge with a binoculars atop torpedo targeting computer and a wheelhouse enclosed by the armored Kalotte.

The large and capable E-boats design was possible through the development of a suitable powerplant. The engines were powerful, compact, robust and lightweight. The boats were adapted to operate in hard combat environments, requiring increases in engine performance to counter the growing weight of armor protection, anti-aircraft weaponry and additional crewmen. M.A.N. and Daimler-Benz builded special lightweight highspeed diesel engines for E-boats development program in the early 1930s, reducing both fire risk and fuel consumption compared to gasoline engines and they based their project on the powerful lightweight engine designs developed for

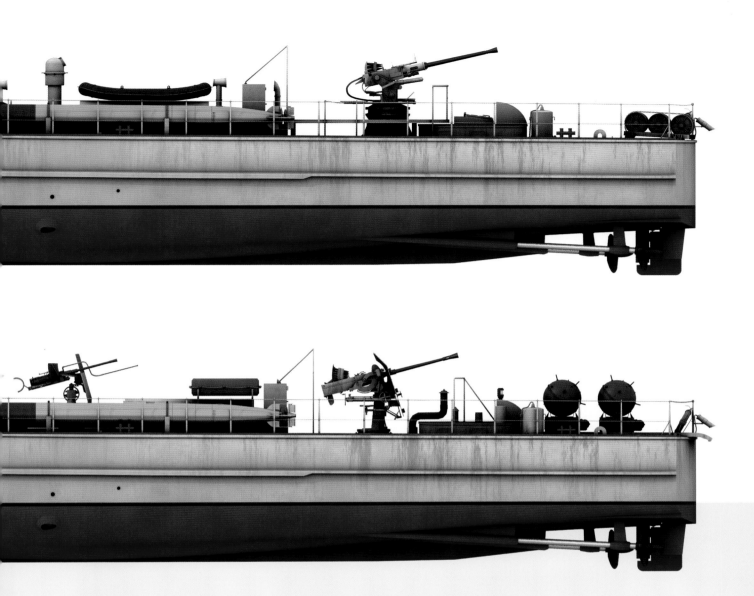

Zeppelins (rigid dirigibles) durind World War One. After many changes and improvements, Daimler-Benz equipped the S38b and S100 classes with the MB511, that has a total output of 7500 hp and could make 43.5 knots (50 mph / 81 kmh) top speed. The engine rooms were spacious and well-ventilated, although noisy; conduits and wiring were neatly laid out to allow accessibility for quick identification and repair; fire risk was diminished by the use of diesel fuel and by a fire extinguishing system; modern instrument panels displayed performance of the three engines and instructions from the bridge were received on miniature engine room telegraphs. These engines were technological marvels and they need delicate hands on the throttle and careful maintenance.

Maintenance was often a matter of life or death: major repairs were undertaken at shore bases or E-boats tenders, but crews had to perform routine maintenance themselves at sea.

S100 class was also fitted up with the RZA5 torpedo targeting director, mounted at the center of the bridge. A dark round ventilator cover hangs on the bridge side above a life ring holder. The Ha-Jü S100 E-boat was field modified to include additional voice pipes to below decks positions and a helmet rack. A machine gun pintle and an oval hand grip are located on the Kalotte's starboard aft edge.

Captains and lookouts of E-boats used the Zeiss 7x50 binoculars mounted onto the torpedo targeting computer while scanning the horizon. This set of precision optics was robust for sea duty and optimal for night use.

Armaments

The E-boats' main battery consisted of two 53,3 cm (21inch) torpedo tubes mounted on the bow and they use to go to action with one torpedo in each tube. Cradles for up to four extra torpedoes were mounted on the deck of later classes, but two was the normal reserve load. Reserve torpedoes were less frequently carried in aereas such as the English Channel, where the Allies employed effective countermeasures. Their weight adversely affected performance, especially in boats like S38b and S100 who had the armored Kalotte, and the hit-and-run tactics rarely allowed the five minutes it took a well-trained crew to reload a tube.

The main armament of S-38b consisted of two 53,3 cm forward torpedo tubes, which could be kept loaded, so, using the four external cradles, the total equipment could be six torpedoes, even if, normally, more than four were not loaded; especially on the units that had the protected bridge (the Kalotte), the reserve torpedoes were almost never transported to save weight. Normally, the torpedoes were the 1528 kg G7a, but from June 1944 were added the 2216 kg large T 3D Dackel and the 1497 kg acoustic autoguide T 5a Zaunkönig. The G7a torpedo was 7,16m (23,5 ft) long and 53,3 cm in diameter, weighed 1528 kg (3369 pounds) including a 320 kg (706 pounds) Hexanite warhead. They had a range of 7.500 mt (8.202 yards) at 40 knots (46 mph / 74 kmh) and 12.000 mt (13.670 yards) at 30 knots (35 mph / 56 kmh).

The E-boats were forced to deal with increasingly strong Allied countermeasures as World War Two progressed, included growing Allied air superiority and british gunboats built specifically to combat the German Schnellboote.

The secondary armament normally included a 20mm MG C/38 Rheinmetall gun, hand-training from a prow position, with Drehkranzlafette 41 installation; on some units there was also a Flakvierling installation with four weapons which, however, required no less than 7-8 gunners.

Abaft there was the location for a 40mm swedish Bofors Flak 28 gun, that needs 7 gunners crew. This weapon was sometimes fitted with armored shields for protection against light projectiles and shrapnel. The gun weighed approximately 521 kg (1.149 pounds) and had a rate of fire of 128 rounds per minute. Its maximum range was 10.000 mt (32.808 ft) and it could be fired in either semi-automatic or automatic mode, used a foot pedal trigger.

In the center of the ship there was a Zwillingsockel 36 (twin pedestal) which mounted two 7,92 mm Mauser MG 34 machine guns in a light, manually- operated anti-aircraft turret. Its advantages were its small size, enabling it to fit between the large ventilator trunks amidships above the engine room, its light weight, and its crew requirement of only one or two.The Mg34 had a muzzle velocity of 755 m (2.477 ft) per second, a cyclic firing rate of 800 to 900 rounds per minute and a maximum horizontal range of 4.570 mt (4.998 yards).

In the armament of S38b were included also 8 depth bombs, hand grenades available to the crew for boarding parties, signal flares which were stowed in a box just aft of the bridge cockpit, and mines of various types.

The open hatchway aft of 2 cm C/38 cannon, mounted in the foredeck of S-38b, provides access to the senior ratings' quarters. The small open hatch, immediately forward of the bridge, leads to the radio and captain's quarters at starboard. The position gave the gunner C/38 a good field of fire and some protection.

S100 class were armed with two 53.3 cm (21 inch) torpedo tubes in the upper hull and one or two torpedoes were usually provided for each tube, depending on the situation, with one in the tube and reloads in the first rack aft of the tubes. The bow-mountes 2 cm cannon was retained, but secondary armament was upgraded to 3.7 cm weapon. Engine room skylights and other unnecessary fittings were removed for simplication of the general arrangements.

On the S-100s class, the location of S38b 40mm swedish Bofors Flak 28 gun, was taken by a turret with a quick-firing 3.7 cm Flak LM/42 weapon. The turret was specifically designed for shipboard use against attacking aircraft. It was a shielded weapon that could be fully operated by only three or four gunners. With a properly trained loader feeding the five-round ammunition clips, it could maintain uninterrupted fire of 190 rounds per minute. It entered service in 1943 and had a 6.400 mt (20.997 ft) range at 45° and anti-aircraft ceiling of 4.800 mt (15.748 ft). Its arc of fire was -10 to + 90° in the vertical plane and the mount had a 360° traverse. The mount including the armored shield weighed approximately 1.350 kg (2.976 pounds).

Two large smoke generators, used for escape and evasion, were stowed in ready positions on the aft deckhouses of the S100 class. Each of these was capable of delivering a thick cloud or grey smoke for up to half an hour. They could be dropped overboard to establish a static smoke screen or to mark a position.

S100 class E-boats were built from mid 1943 until World War Two's conclusion in May of 1945.

These units were equipped with efficient hydrophones, a sensitive directional microphone array mounted outside the hull below the waterline, and were extremely effective. Hidrophones were able to locate a PT boat travelling at 30 knots (35mph / 56 kmh) from a range of 18 km. They were effective even while underway and emitted no telltail signals to the enemy.

Schnellboot S38B, 1942.
Top view..

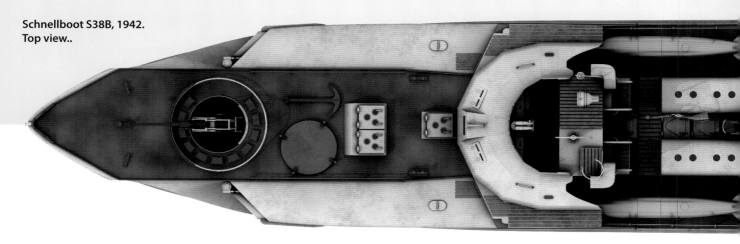

Schnellboot S100, 1943.
Top view..

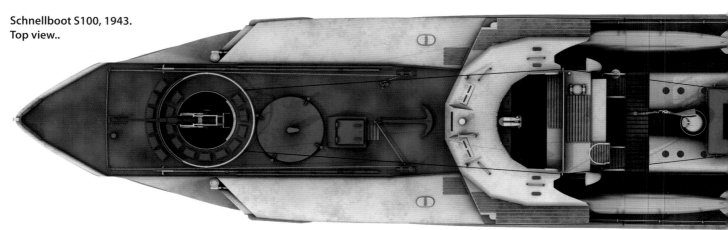

Even if E-boats usually operated at night in formations and communications was vital to navigation, formation keeping, target location, and attack coordination, rarely were fitted with radar, as they normally operated in continuous radio contact with discovery ground stations, but hidrophones performance was degraded as the detecting vessels' speed increased.

Service and conclusion

E-boats operated in the English Channel, intercepting ships heading to English ports in the south and east, and in the Baltic, North Sea, Barents Sea, Mediterranean, Black Sea, scraped there by ground and / or river transport, where they served as auxiliaries of large cruise ships. Rarely they were used as U-Boot Provisioners.

E-boats entered into action on 10 May 1940, when they seriously damaged the destroyer HMS Kelly, and on the night between 20 and 21 June they began their activity against the British merchant traffic. Soon the sailors began to talk about "E-Boats Alley", because, above all to divert the air units of the RAF from the air defense, the German motorboats attacked incessantly and in broad daylight. The situation changed when even the British were able to put into the sea a force of torpedo boats and gunboats. However, the E-boats continued to fight fiercely until the end of the conflict and, together with the submarines, were the last to surrender.

The Schnellboote of the Kriegsmarine had as main targets the allied convoys and, during the Second World War, about 230 units sank 101 merchant ships for a total of 214.728t. However, there were also military targets and the crews were awarded the destruction of 12 destroyers, 11 mine-sweepers, 8 units for amphibious operations, 6 moto torpedo boats, a torpedo boat, two gunboats, a mine-layer and a submarine. Considerable results were also achieved with mines: 37

merchants for a total of 148.535 tons, a destroyer, two mine-sweepers and four landing units. They damaged two cruisers, five destroyers, two frigates, three landing ships, a repair ship, nVl tug amd many merchant vessels.

In all, the sinking of 187 enemy ships can be ascribed to the work of the Schnellboote.

E-boats service produced twentythree Knight's Cross winners, eight of whom were further distinguished with the Oak Leaves, and 112 Deutsches Kreuz (German Cross) in Gold winners.

Among the successes of the fleet of Captain of the ship Rudolf Petersen, Führer des Schnellboote (commander of the torpedo boats), there is also the ally set-back of Slapton Sands in the night between 27 and 28 April 1944, when two American landing units were sunk and a third one was damaged, with the death of 639 Americans who were training for D-Day.

The S-204 of the 4. Schnellbootsflotille, whose crew handed over himself to the Royal Navy on 13 May 1945, was the last German naval unit to accept the surrender.

Three boats, the S-130 (renamed P5230), the S-208 (P5208) and the S-212 (P5212) were retained for evidence. The P5230 and P5208 were used for clandestine intelligence operations in the Baltic, until 1957, in a unit commanded by John Harvey-Jones.

During the Spanish Civil War, Germany delivered to the insurgent forces the obsolete Schnellboot from S-1 to S-5.2 and during the conflict sold 6 units of the S-38 class to Spain, and the possibility of building them under license. Once the dispute was over, another 6 units of type S-38 were built with the support of Lürssen.

Spain also, after the Second World War, used some S-38 units that operated in the waters of the Straits of Gibraltar.

The poor seaworthiness of the Italian-designed MAS boats of World War I and early World War II led its navy to build its own version of E-boats, the CRDA 60 t type, classed MS. The prototype was designed

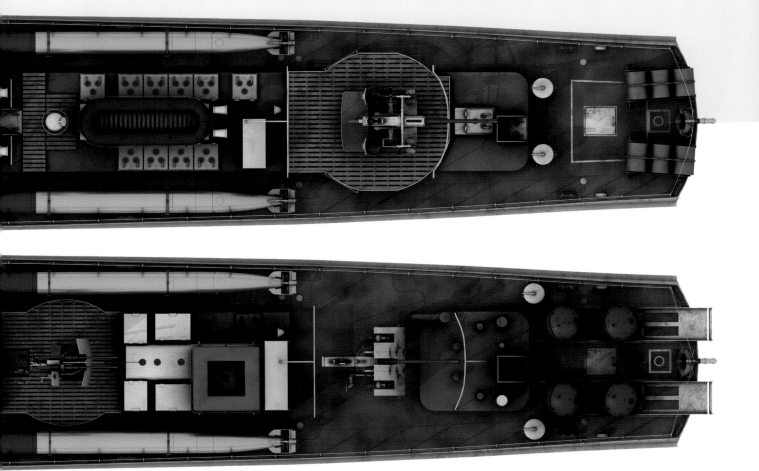

GENERAL CHARACTERISTICS

Class and type:	S38b
Displacement:	92,5 tons (84 mt) standard, 115 tons (104 mt) full loaded
Length:	35 m (114 ft – 10 in)
Beam:	5,1 m (16 ft 9 in)
Draught:	1,5 m (5 ft)
Powerplant:	three 2200 hp Daimler-Benz MB 511 12-cylinder, inline, liquid-cooled engines
Speed:	39,5 knots (73 km/h; 46 mph)
Range:	700 nmi (1297 km; 806 mi) at 35 knots (65 km/h; 40 mph)
Armament:	two 53.3 cm (21 inch) torpedo tubes with four G7a, T3d or T5a torpedoes in the upper bow
	one 2 cm Rhein-metall MG C/38 cannon in bow
	two 7.92mm MG34 machine guns in one Zwillingsockel 36 amidships
	one 2 cm MG C/30 or C/38 or one 4cm Bofors Flak 28 cannon on aft deck
Crew:	21 to 30

**Schnellboot S38B, 1942.
Front view.**

on the pattern of six German-built E-boats captured from the Yugoslav Navy in 1941. Two of them sank the British light cruiser HMS Manchesterin August 1942, the largest victory by fast torpedo craft in the Second World War. After the war these boats served with the Italian Navy, some well into the 1970s.

At present, only one boat is preserved, the S-130. It is maintained with private funds, but is in the care of the British Military Powerboat Trust of Southampton. This particular boat participated on October 21, 1943 in the "Exercise Tiger".

Schnellboot force served honorably and the German military won many decorations for their work, denoted by a badge depicting an E-boat passing through a wreath. The standard for granting them was good behavior, showing up for their actions and participating in at least twelve operations against the enemy. It could also be given for a particular event, such as the sinking of a boat or special circumstances.

An example is the Captain Walter Knopp who painted his personal insignia (ALTER) on the Kalotte of his S38b vessel. The 8th flotilla, who belongs his E-boat, operated in the North Sea and English Channel areas throughout the war.

One of the peculiarities of E-boats was the power of the engines. Daimler-Benz improved the performances of these vessels producing many type of engines and at the end of the wartime they produced the MB518 with 3300 hp.

As E-boats communication was vital to navigation, formation keeping, target location, and attack coordination, towards the end of 1943, a Schnellboote was fitted with a FuMo 71 Liechtenstein B/C

Back view.

radar, derived from aeronautics. This was a fixed radar array measuring approximately 1.3 mt (4.3 ft) by 1.6 mt (5.2 ft) that could scan a 35° arc ahead the boat. Its range was limited to 2.6 km (1.237 miles) but it was very accurate for ranging and useful for navigating in darkness and fog.

On the contrary, after the war, the German torpedo boats could be supplied with different types of passive discovery systems, based on the interception of enemy radar emissions, such as the FuMB Ant 3 Bali 1, the FuMB 32 Flores, the FuMB 24 Cuba 1a, the FuMB 23 and 28 Naxos or the FuMB 26 Tunis. A type FuG/VaU receiver/transmitter provided high frequency ship – to –shore radio communication, general reception and long range communication. It was mounted in the radio room forward and below the wheelhouse, which served also as the radioman's quarters. Another radioman operated a short range Very High Frequency (VHF) type Lo 1 UK 35 voice transmitter receiver in the wheelhouse, that enabled fast communications between other boats in the flottilla.

E-boats was an investiment in the concept that quality and skill will outclass mass production on the battlefield. This was tactically correct, but it did not account the strategic strain on Germany's manifacturing and fighting capabilities over the course of a lenghty two-front war.

Bibliography

"Schnellboot in action" – T. Garth Connelly and David L. Krakow

GENERAL CHARACTERISTICS

Class and type:	S100
Displacement:	92,5 tons (84 mt) standard, 115 tons (104 mt) full loaded
Length:	35 m (114 ft – 10 in)
Beam:	5,1 m (16 ft 9 in)
Draught:	1,5 m (5 ft)
Powerplant:	three 2500 hp Daimler-Benz MB 511 12-cylinder, inline, liquid-cooled engines
Speed:	42 knots (78 km/h; 48 mph)
Range:	700 nmi (1297 km; 806 mi) at 35 knots (65 km/h; 40 mph)
Armament:	two 53.3 cm (21 inch) torpedo tubes with four G7a, T3d or T5a torpedoes in the upper bow,
	one 2 cm Rheinmetall MG C/38 cannon in bow,
	two 2 cm MG C/38 cannon in a Zwillinglafette amidships,
	one 4 cm Bofors Flak 28 cannon or one 3.7 cm Rheinmetall Borsig Flak M42 cannon on the aft deck
Crew:	21

**Schnellboot S100, 1943.
Front view.**

Back view.

Schnellboot S38B, 1942.

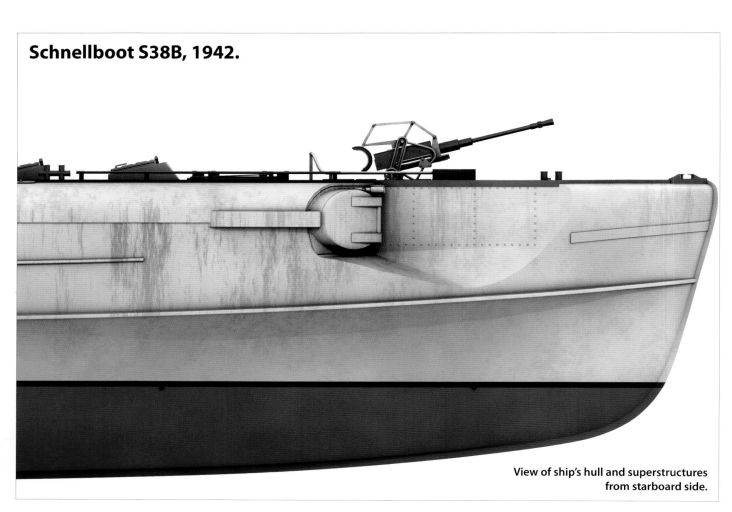

View of ship's hull and superstructures
from starboard side.

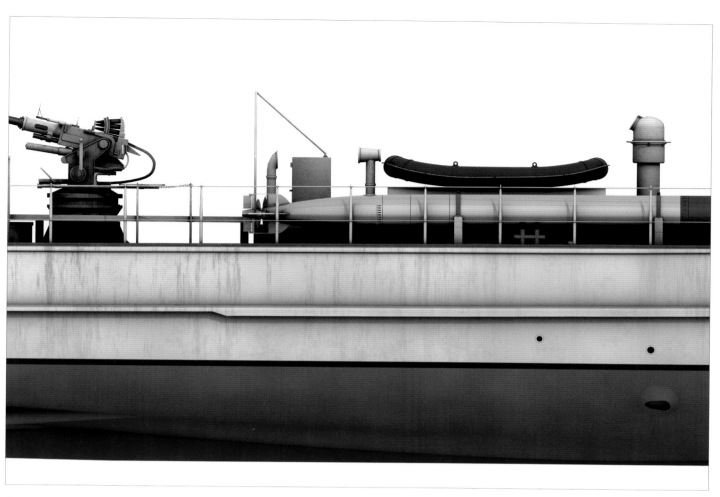

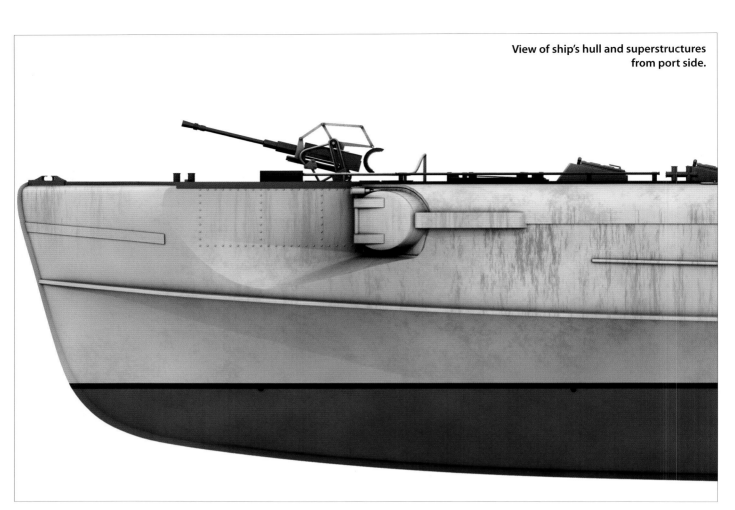

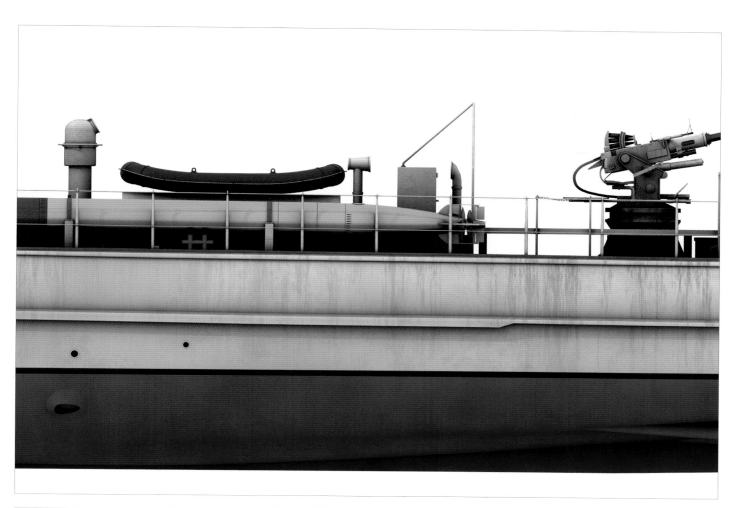

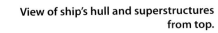

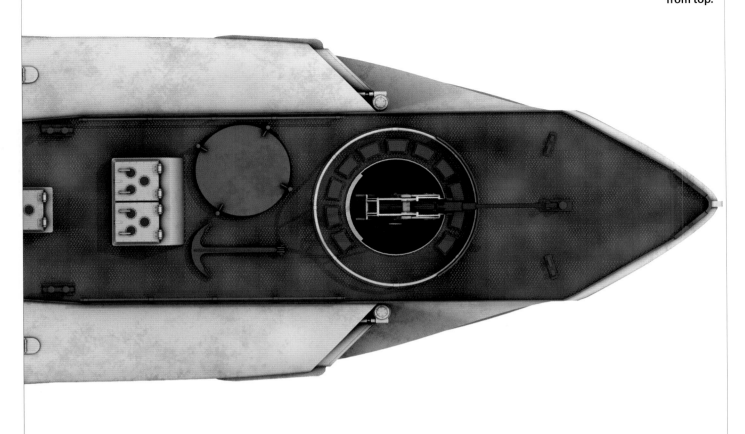

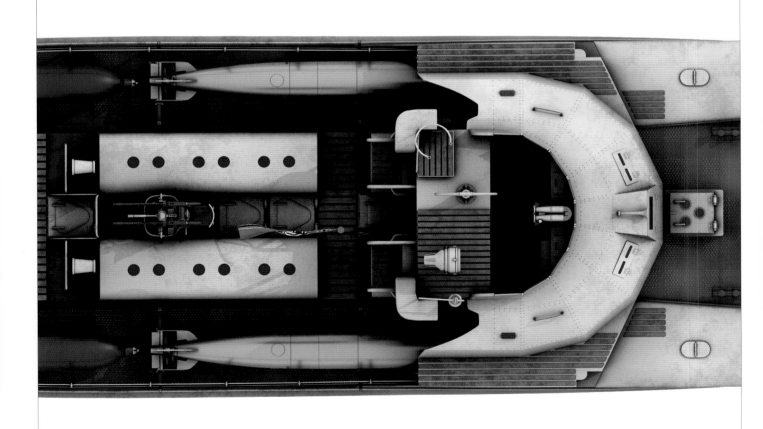

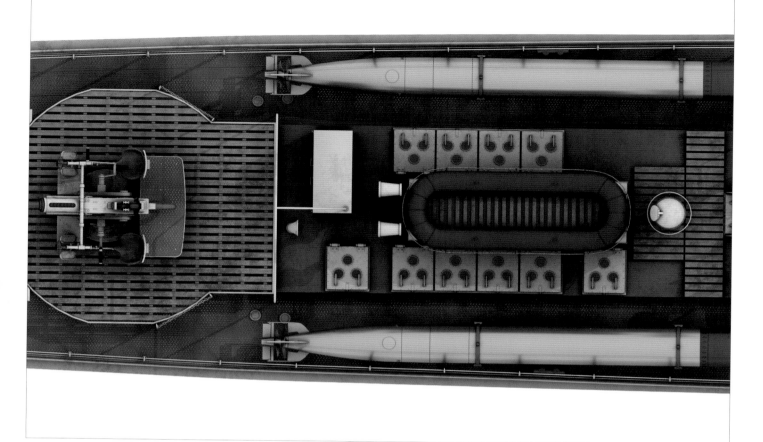

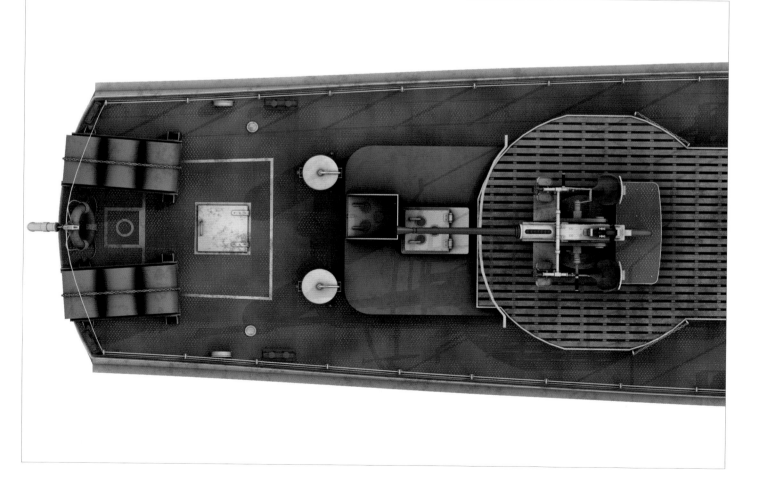

Close view of the Number One (starboard) tube with open and closed door.

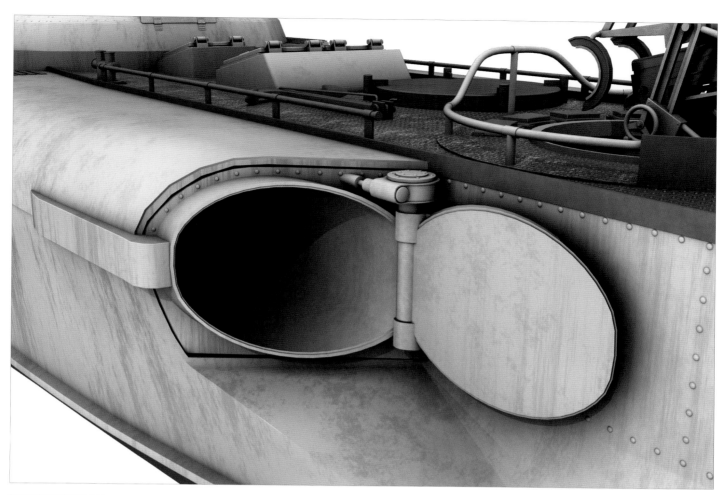

Views of the 20mm Rheinmetall MG C/38 cannon in the bow. This gun had a muzzle velocity of 875 meters per seconds, a horizontal range of about 4900 meters and a vertical range of about 3700 meters.

Views of the 20mm Rheinmetall MG C/38 cannon in the bow. This gun had a muzzle velocity of 875 meters per seconds, a horizontal range of about 4900 meters and a vertical range of about 3700 meters.

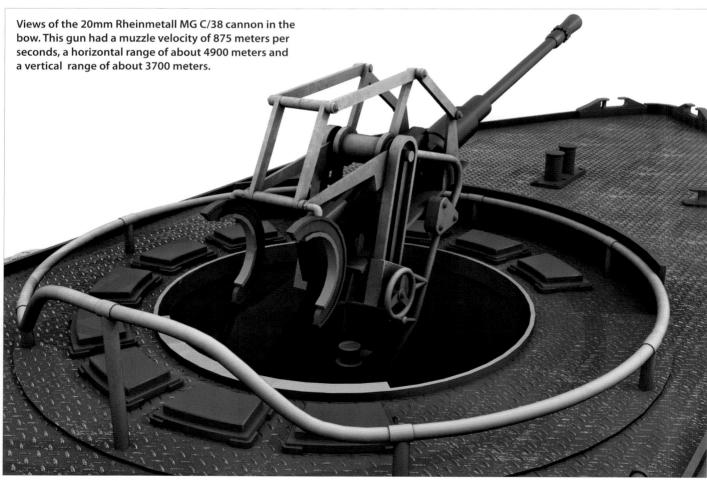

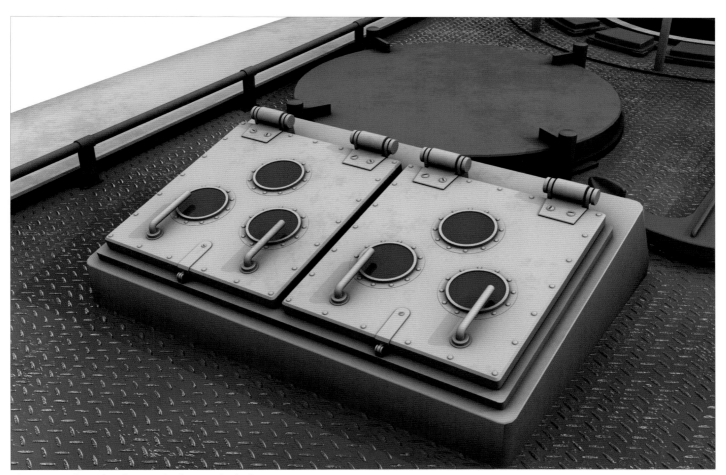

Close view of two hatches on the forecastle deck.

Schnellboot. Type S-38 and S-100

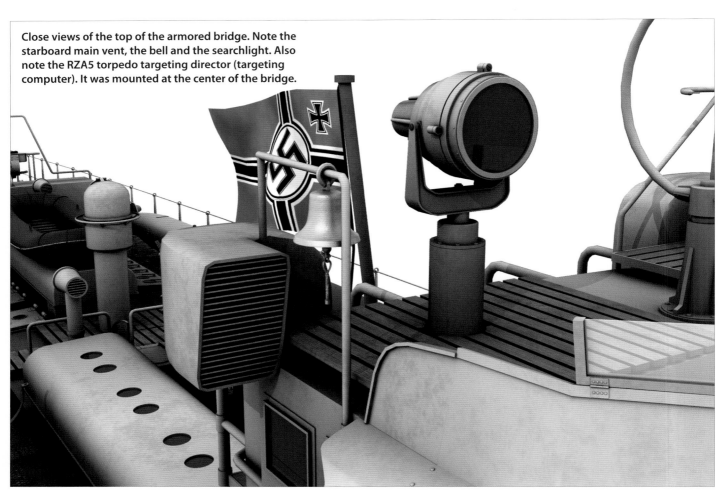

Close views of the top of the armored bridge. Note the starboard main vent, the bell and the searchlight. Also note the RZA5 torpedo targeting director (targeting computer). It was mounted at the center of the bridge.

View of the rear part of the bridge from starboard side. Note the two foot-boards on each side.

View of the rear part of the bridge. Note one of the torpedo inserted into the starboard launch tube.

Overall view of the front part of the
ship from starboard side.

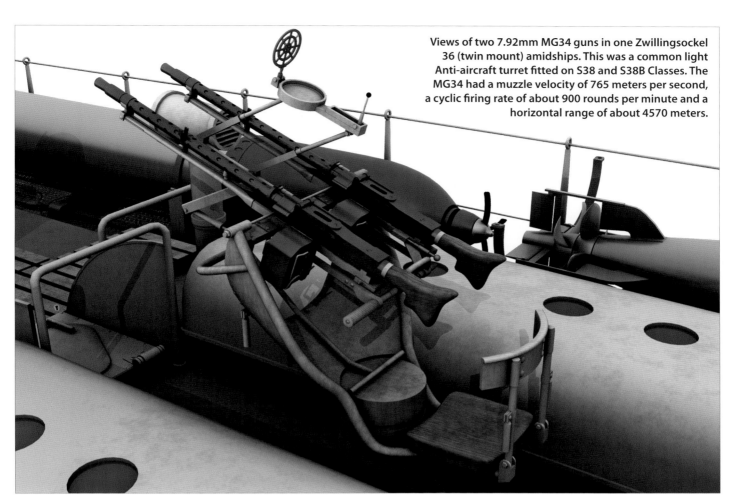

Views of two 7.92mm MG34 guns in one Zwillingsockel 36 (twin mount) amidships. This was a common light Anti-aircraft turret fitted on S38 and S38B Classes. The MG34 had a muzzle velocity of 765 meters per second, a cyclic firing rate of about 900 rounds per minute and a horizontal range of about 4570 meters.

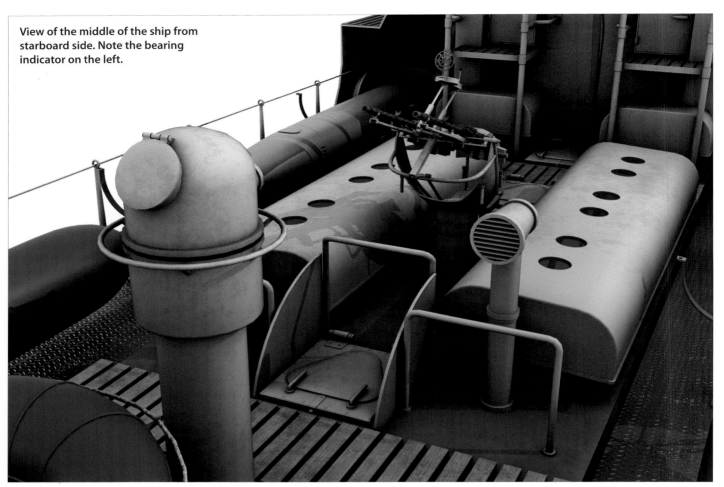

View of the middle of the ship from starboard side. Note the bearing indicator on the left.

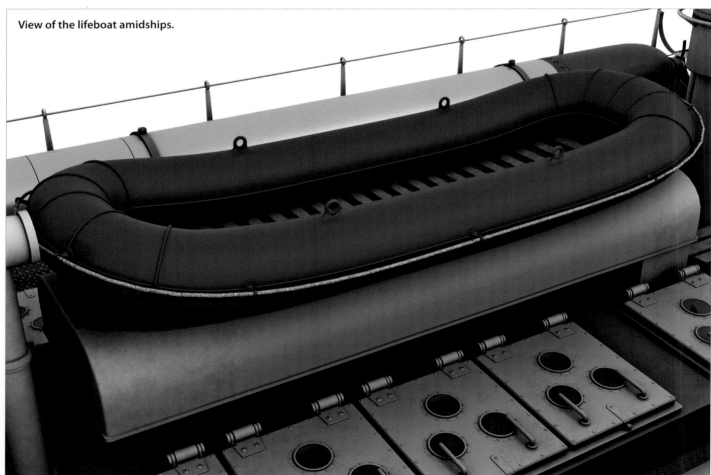

View of the lifeboat amidships.

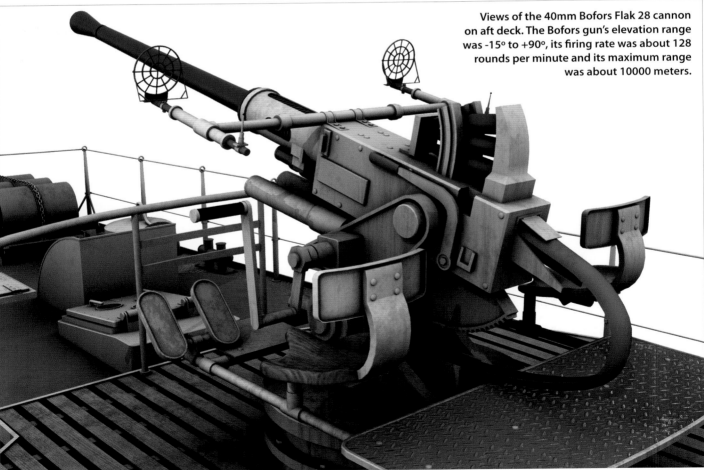

Views of the 40mm Bofors Flak 28 cannon on aft deck. The Bofors gun's elevation range was -15° to +90°, its firing rate was about 128 rounds per minute and its maximum range was about 10000 meters.

View of the aft deck with superstructures. Note the two cylindrical smoke generators.

View of the depth charges at the stern. Each charge was released by manually disconnecting the individual cables that lashed it on the rack. They ranged in weight from 139Kg to 240Kg.

Views of the 40mm Bofors Flak 28 cannon on aft deck from port side.

View of a torpedo from port side.

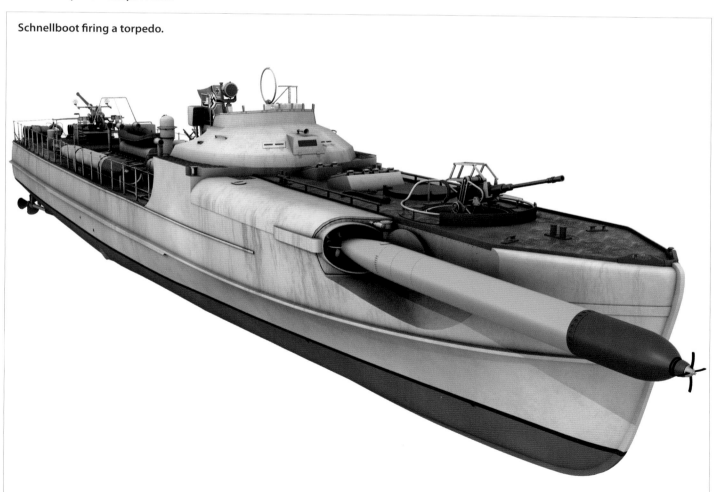

Schnellboot firing a torpedo.

View of the middle of the ship from port side.

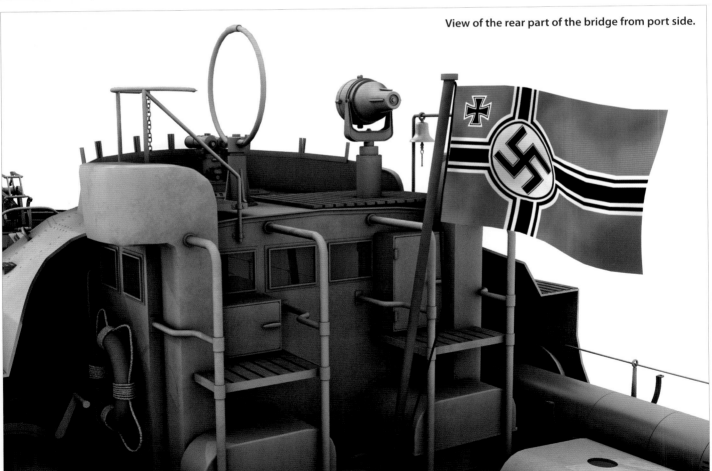

View of the rear part of the bridge from port side.

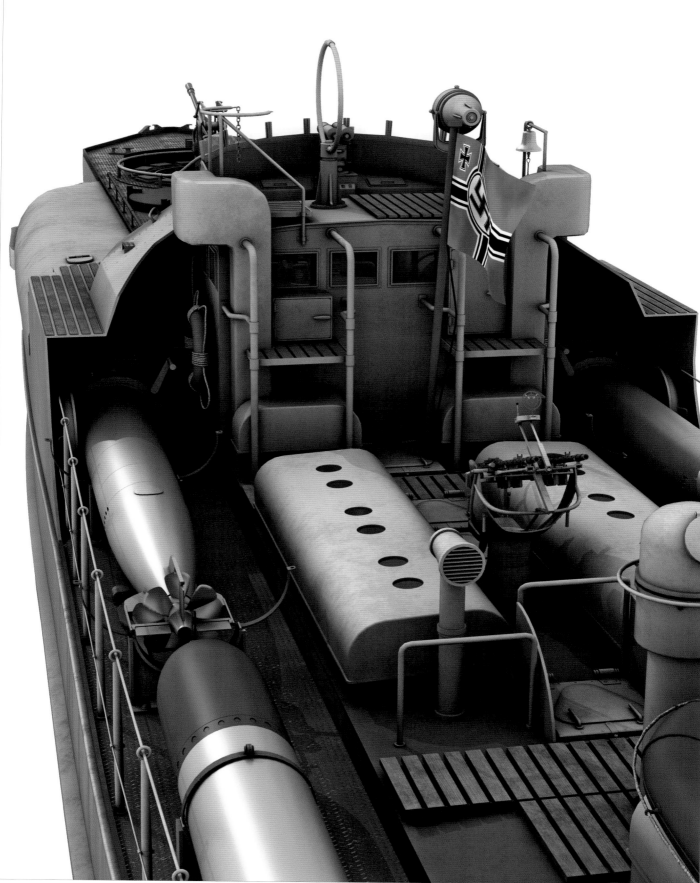

View of the bridge from port side.

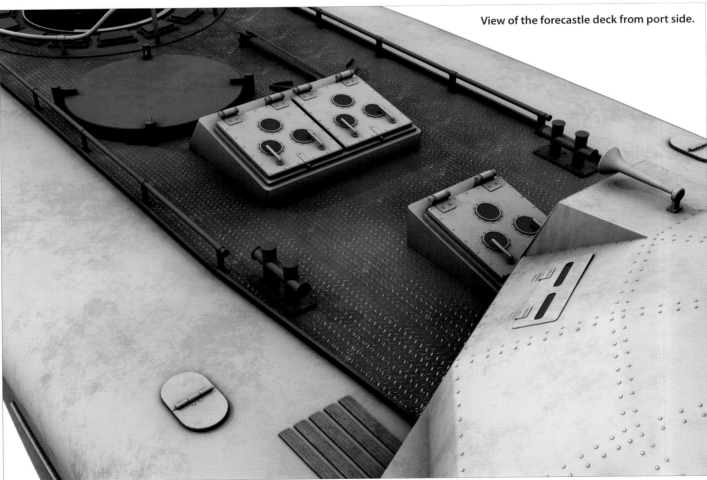

View of the forecastle deck from port side.

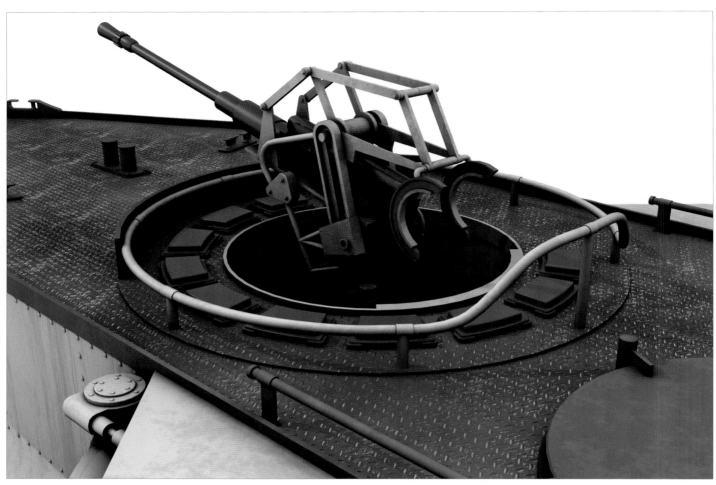

Views of the 20 mm Rheinmetall MG C/38 cannon in the bow from port side.

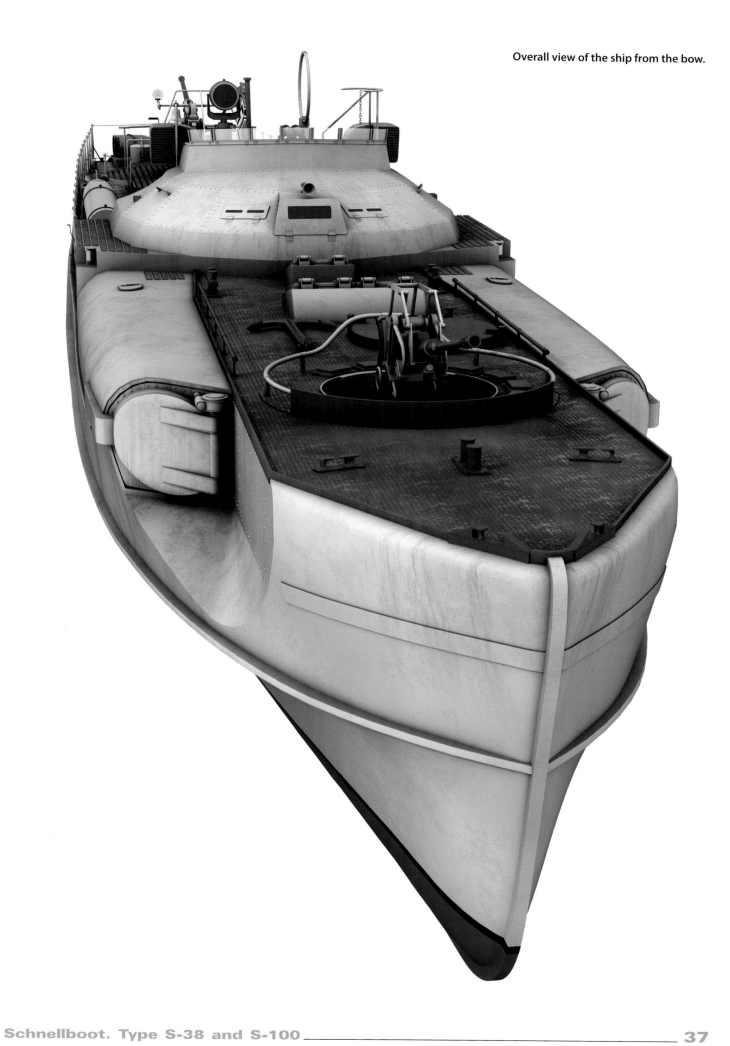

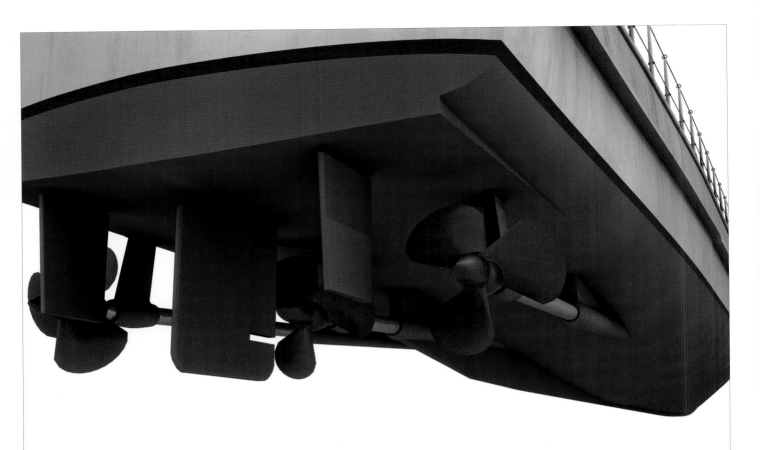

Views of the rudders and propellers area.

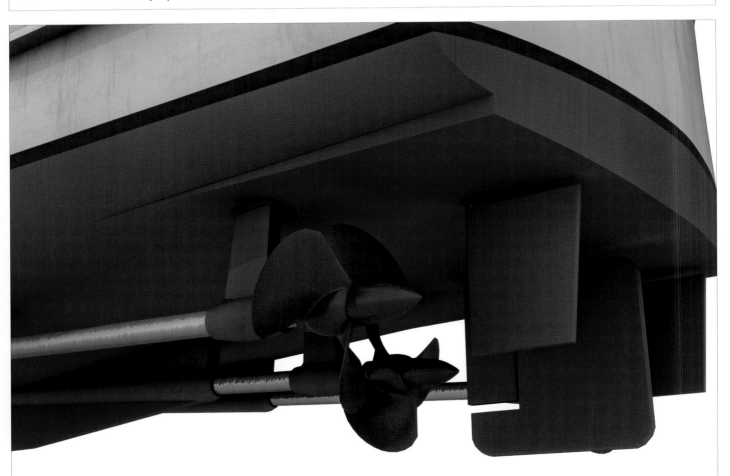

Schnellboot S100, 1943.

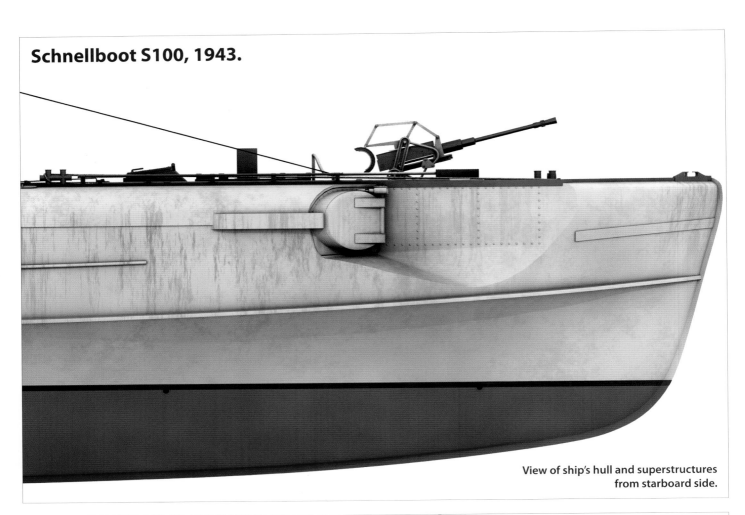

View of ship's hull and superstructures
from starboard side.

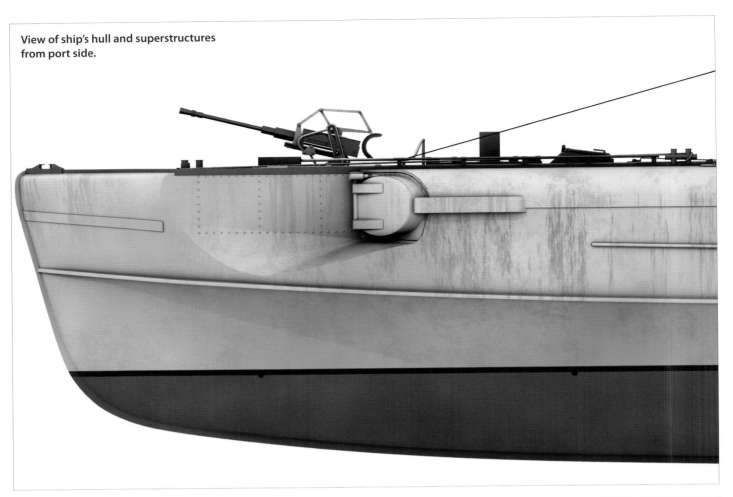

View of ship's hull and superstructures
from port side.

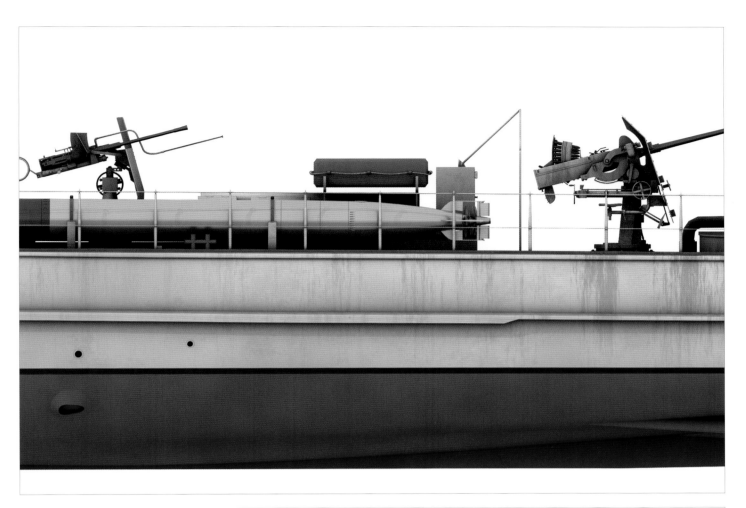

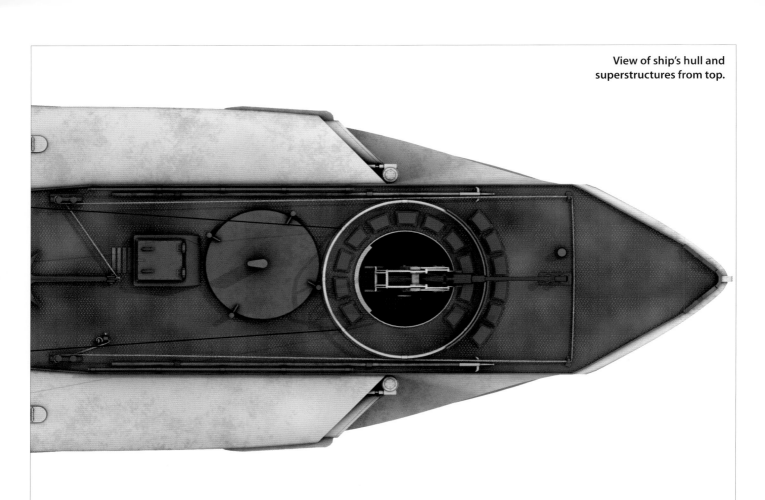

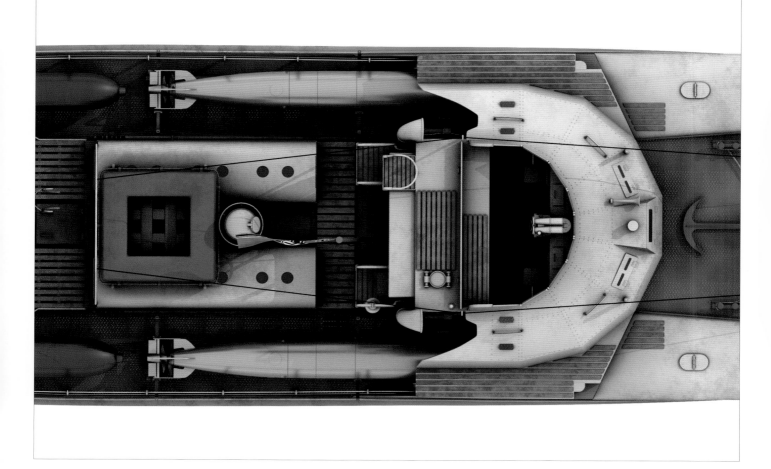

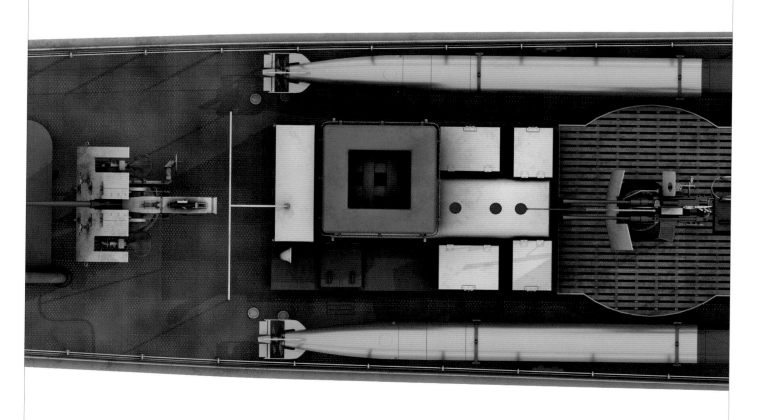

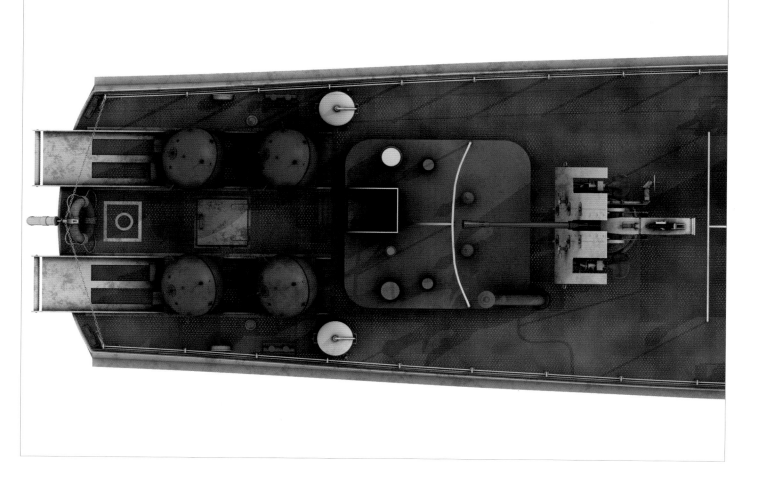

Overall view of the bow.

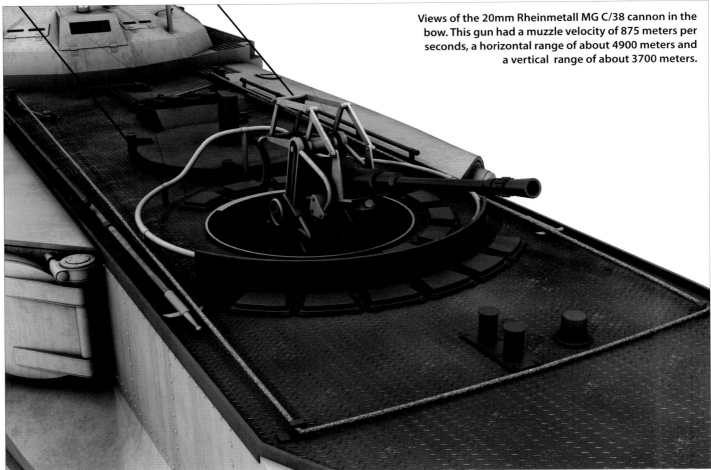

Views of the 20mm Rheinmetall MG C/38 cannon in the bow. This gun had a muzzle velocity of 875 meters per seconds, a horizontal range of about 4900 meters and a vertical range of about 3700 meters.

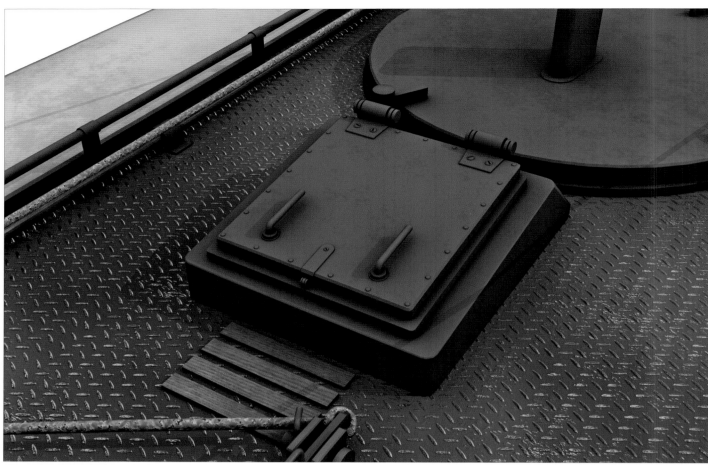

Close view of a hatch on the forecastle deck.

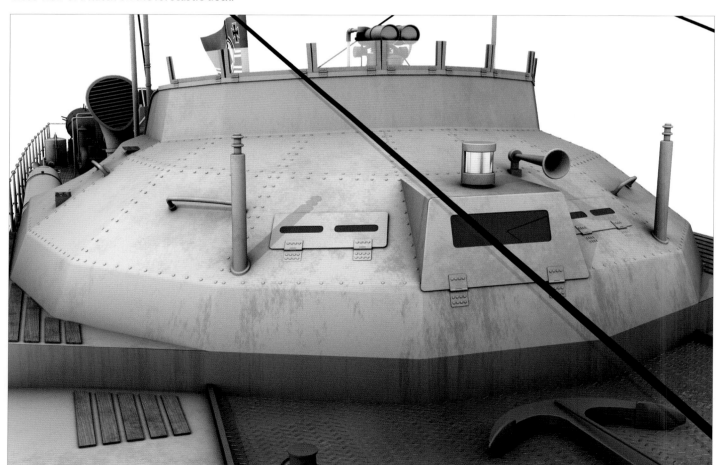

Overall view of the armored bridge.

Close views of the top of the armored bridge. Note the starboard main vent and the RZA5 torpedo targeting director (targeting computer). It was mounted at the center of the bridge.

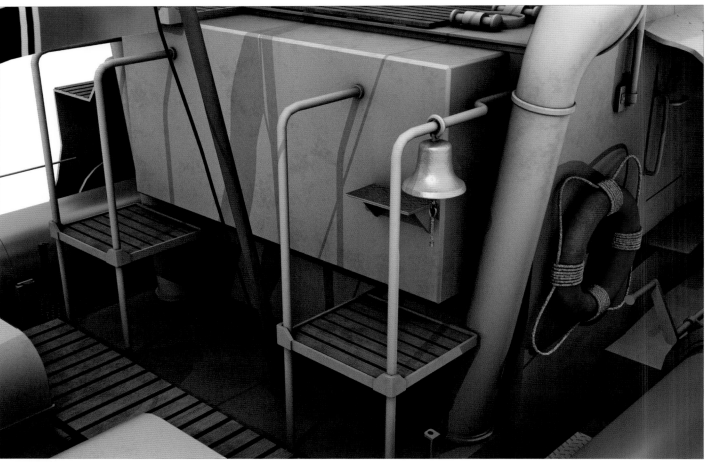

View of the rear part of the bridge from starboard side. Note the two foot-boards on each side.

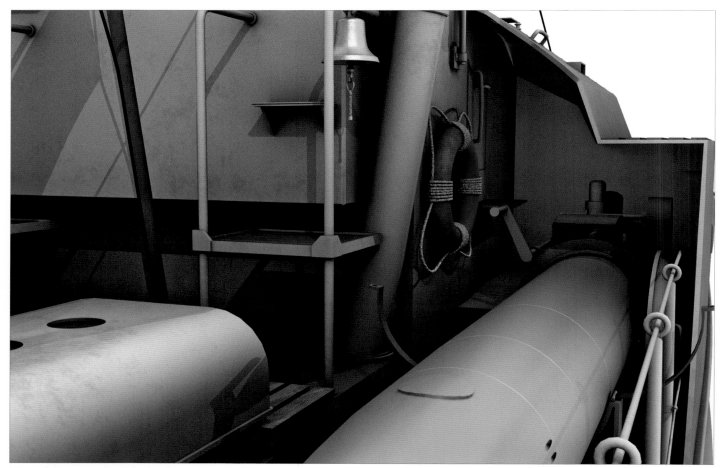

View of the rear part of the bridge. Note one of the torpedo inserted into the starboard launch tube.

Overall view of the front part of the ship from starboard side.

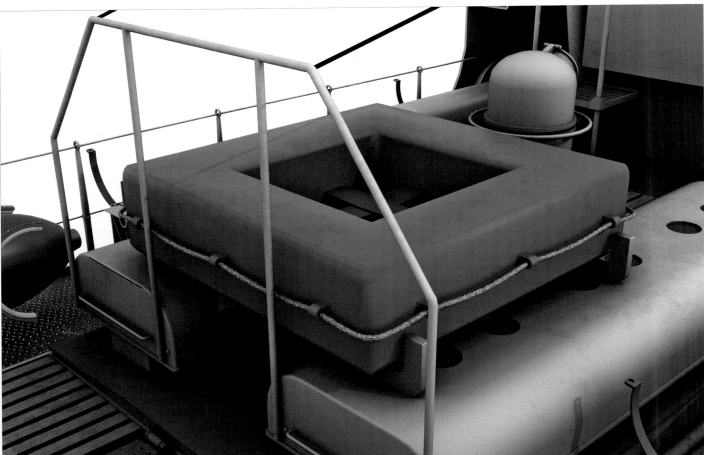

View of one of the lifeboats amidships from starboard side.

Views of two 20mm MG C/38 guns in one Zwillingslafette (twin mount) amidships. It had a cyclic firing rate of about 480 rounds per minute, a muzzle velocity of about 800 meters per second and a range of about 4900 meters at 45° of elevation and 3700 meters at 85° of elevation (anti-aircraft ceiling)

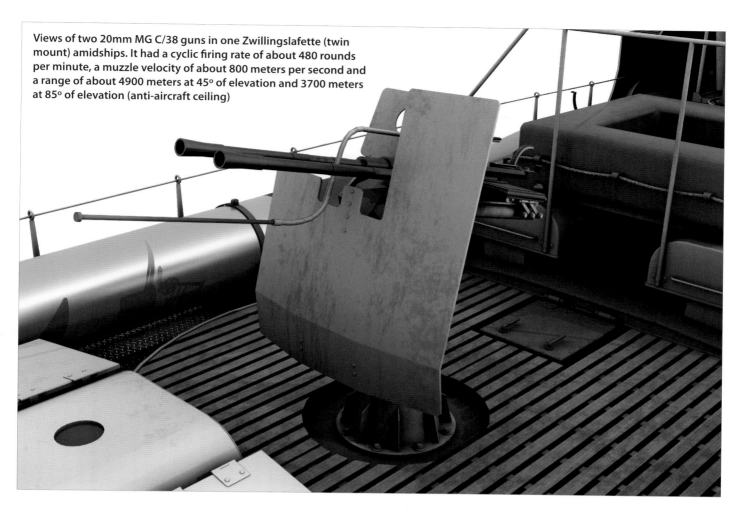

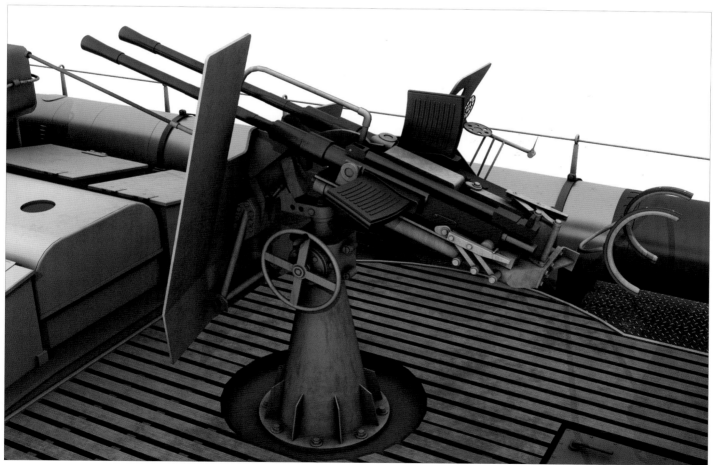

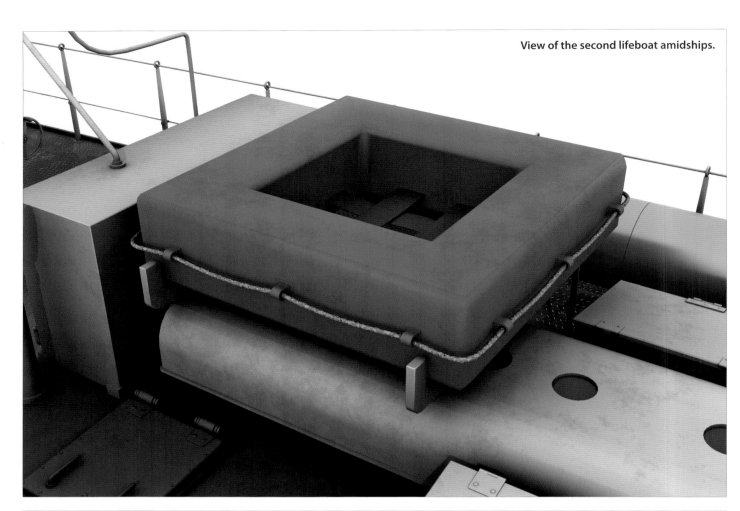

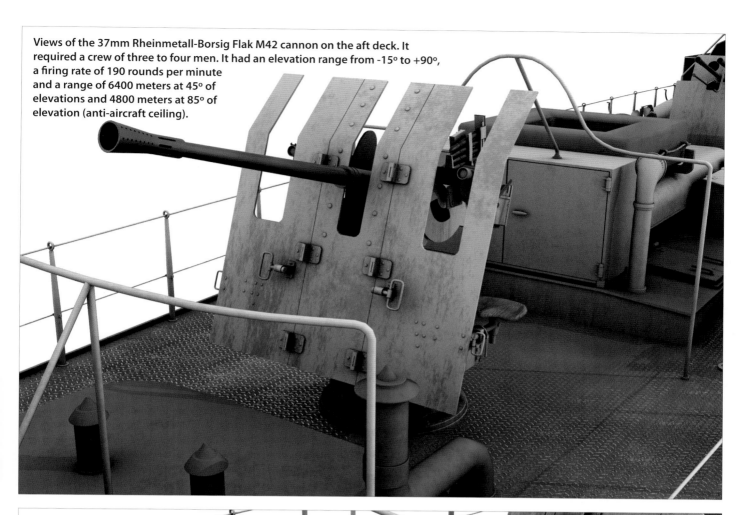

Views of the 37mm Rheinmetall-Borsig Flak M42 cannon on the aft deck. It required a crew of three to four men. It had an elevation range from -15° to +90°, a firing rate of 190 rounds per minute and a range of 6400 meters at 45° of elevations and 4800 meters at 85° of elevation (anti-aircraft ceiling).

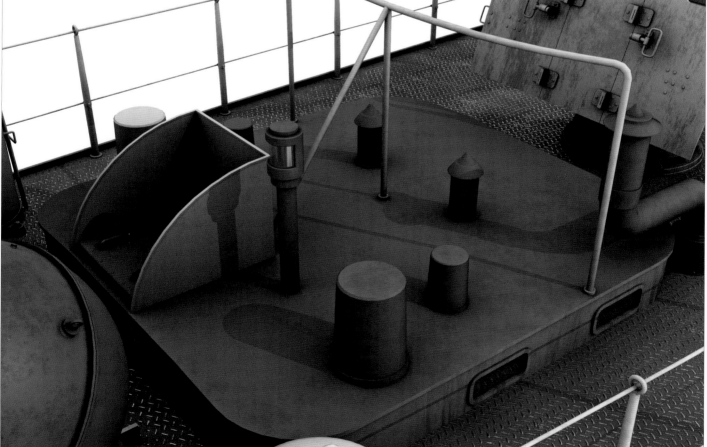

View of the aft deck with superstructures.

Overall view of the rear part of the ship from starboard side.

View of the naval mines at the stern from starboard side.

View of the naval mines at the stern from port side. Note the cylindrical smoke generators.

View of one of the lifeboat from port side.

View of a torpedo from port side.

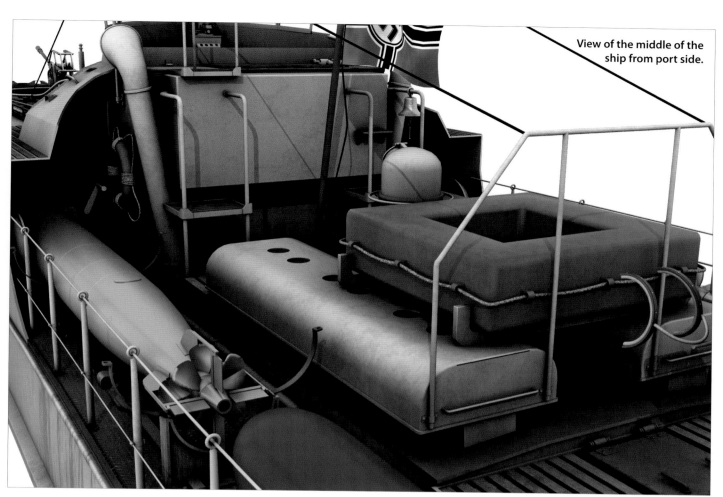

View of the middle of the
ship from port side.

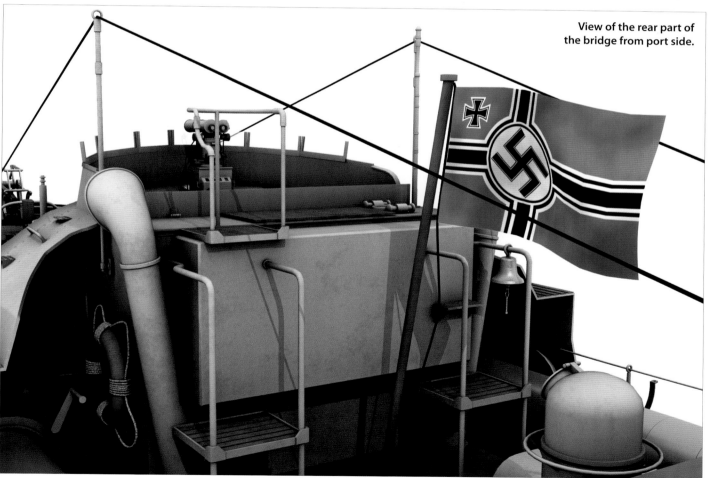

View of the rear part of
the bridge from port side.

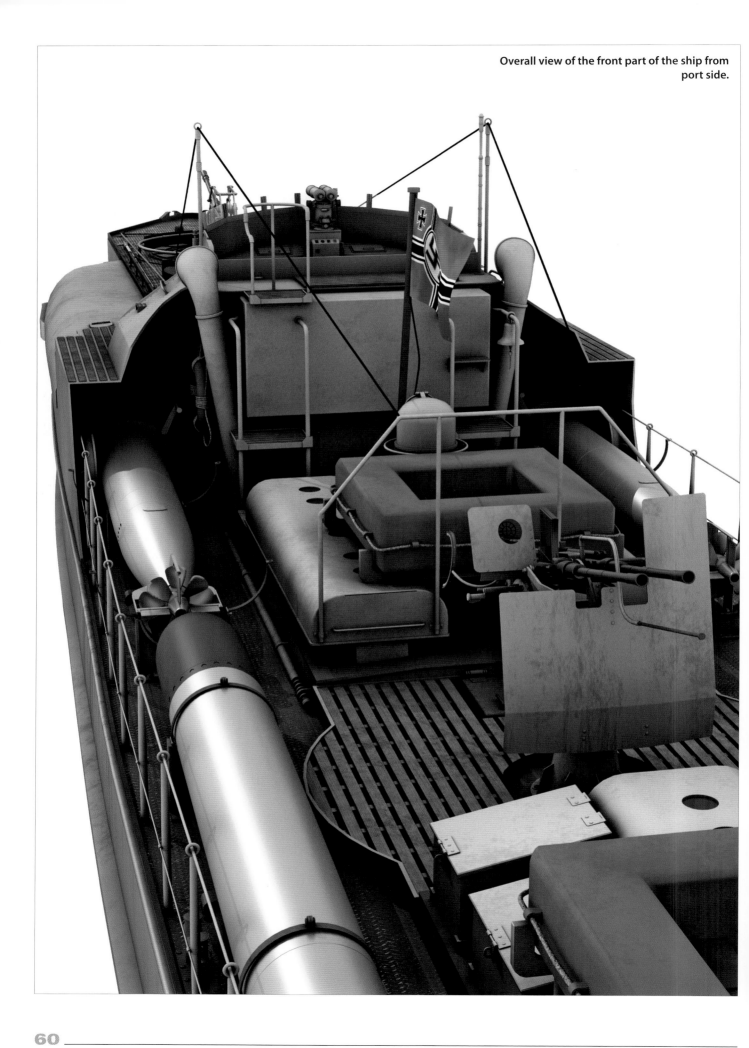

Overall view of the front part of the ship from port side.

Overall view of
the rear part of
the ship from
port side.

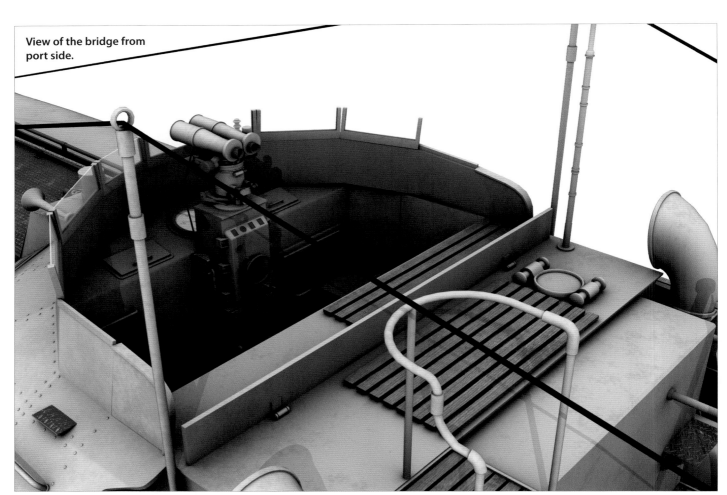

View of the bridge from port side.

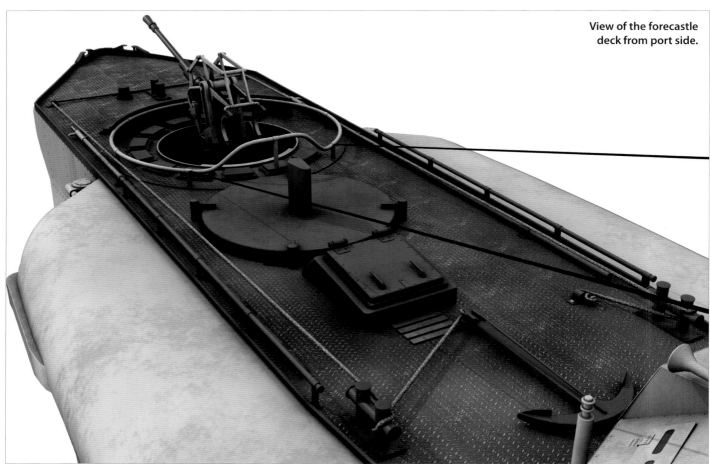

View of the forecastle deck from port side.

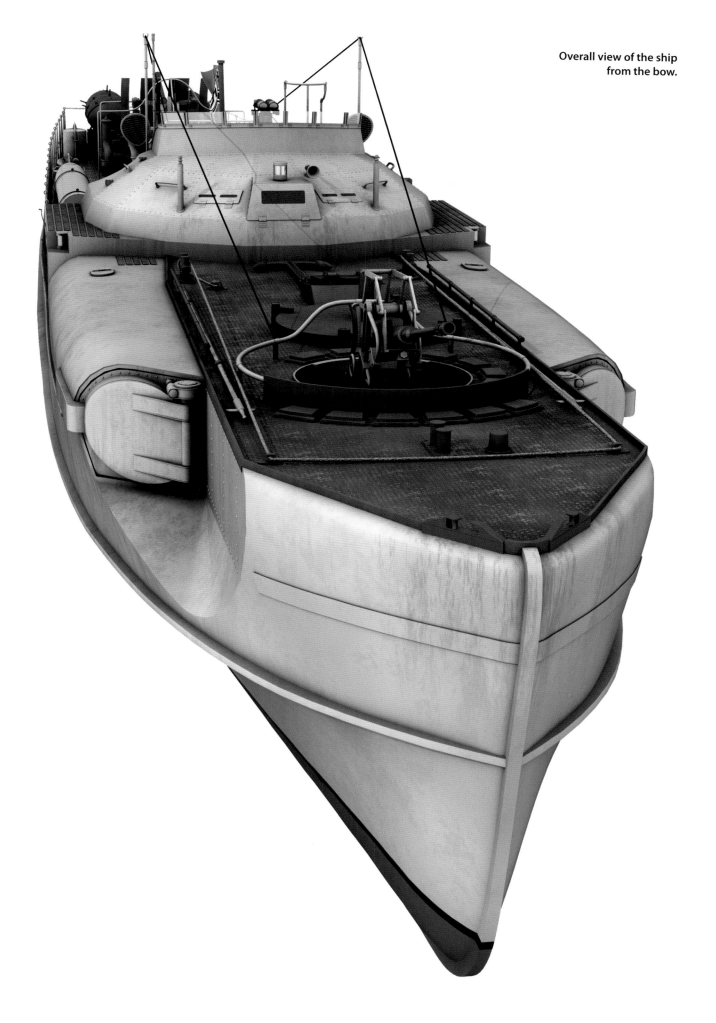

Overall view of the ship
from the bow.

Views of the 20mm Rheinmetall MG C/38 cannon
in the bow from port side.

View of the 37mm
Rheinmetall-Borisg Flak
M42 cannon from port side.

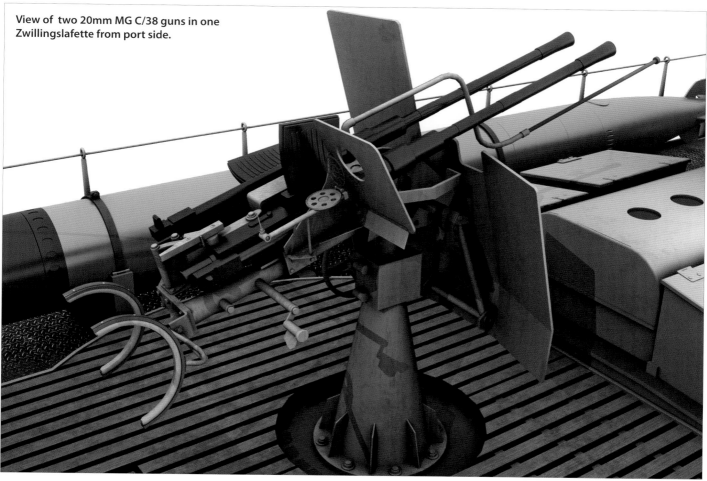

View of two 20mm MG C/38 guns in one
Zwillingslafette from port side.

Overall view of the ship from the stern.

37 mm Flak M42 and 20 mm Flak 38
in firing position.

20 mm Rheinmetall C/38
in firing position.

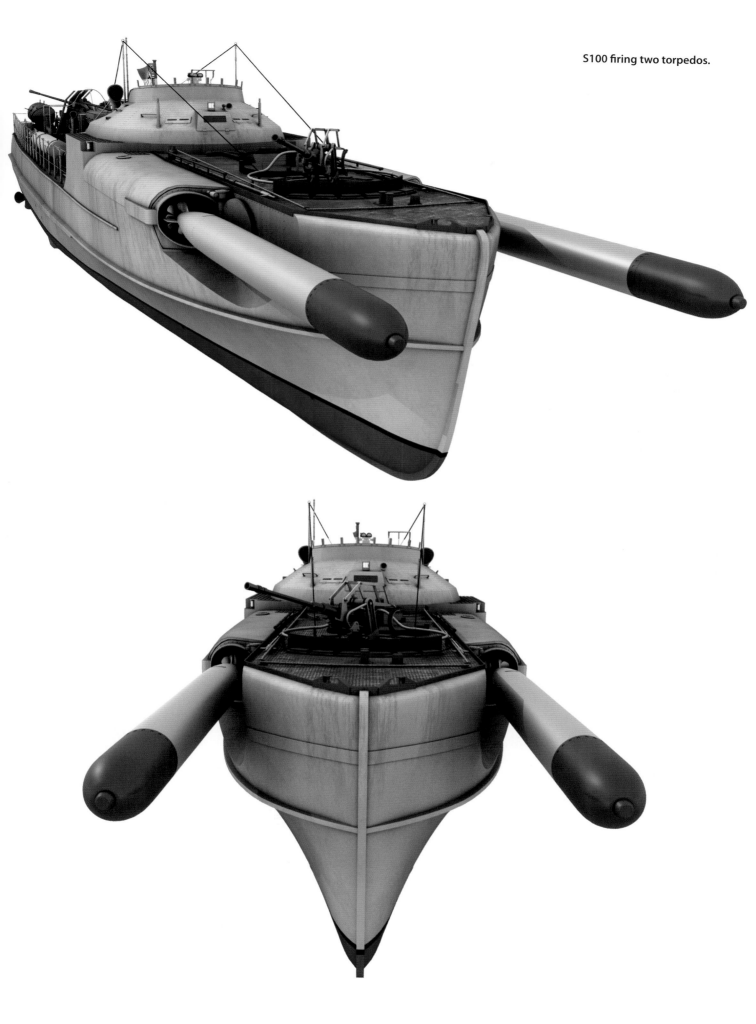

Schnellboot. Type S-38 and S-100

Visit our shop online **shop.kagero.pl**

Schnellboot. Type S-38 and S-100 – Carlo Cestra
LUBLIN 2018 • ISBN 978-83-65437-71-6
© All rights reserved. With the exception of quoting brief passages for the purposes of review, no part of this publication may be reproduced without prior written permission from the Publisher.
3D illustrations and captions, text: **Carlo Cestra** • Design: **KAGERO STUDIO** – Łukasz Maj
KAGERO Publishing • www.kagero.pl, e-mail: kagero@kagero.pl, marketing@kagero.pl
Editorial office, Marketing, Distribution: KAGERO Publishing, Akacjowa 100, os. Borek, Turka, 20-258 Lublin 62, Poland, phone/fax (+48) 81 501 21 05
w w w . k a g e r o . e u